HECATE
THE
BANDICOOT

HECATE
THE
BANDICOOT

JANET LITTLE

DODD, MEAD & COMPANY · NEW YORK

1   2   3   4   5   6   7   8   9   10

ISBN: 0-396-07893-1
Library of Congress Catalog Card Number: 80-69437

For
SLOAN
and
ALEX
and the
RANDALL CLAN

HECATE
THE
BANDICOOT

Hecate the bandicoot
Slavered at the maw.
Hecate was hungry,
And she wanted something raw.

Thick and swarmy was the night,
Addled was the air.
Smelly was that bandicoot,
Matted was her hair.

Guavas thudded to the earth,
Lorises were yawling.
Somewhere in the eel grass
Hecate was crawling.

Mealybugs and earwigs
Fainted from the heat.
Hecate consumed them,
And thought of redder meat.

Fanny Thimble flounced along,
Orchids for to find.
Hecate was worming,
Sweatily, behind.

Dimpled were her rosy knees,
Frilly were her socks.
Hecate the feculent
Hid behind some rocks.

"Lackadaisy! Lackaday!
What a precious dear!"
Fanny seized that bandicoot,
And kissed its wormy ear.

"You, my sweet, will be my pet,
My very special friend.
We'll play Acey-Deucy,
And Catch and Let's Pretend."

Fanny took the balding tail,
And tied it to her thumb.
She dragged her through the underbrush,
And showed her to her mum.

"If you want to keep it, dear,
You must delouse its coat."
So Fanny scrubbed her beast in bleach,
And hugged it by the throat.

Fanny made her bandicoot
A frock with poplin pockets.
She decked her out in diadems,
And moa plumes, and lockets.

And to this day, that bandicoot
Is smelling like a crocus,
While sitting on a windowseat,
And staring out of focus.